OVERCOMING CI
EMOTIONAL DEPRIVATION

Overcoming the Pain of Unavailable Parents: A
Practical Guide to Healing and Self-Discovery

Victory Jensen

INTRODUCTION

Childhood Emotional Deprivation

Neglected children internalize a central message that conveys their insignificance and unworthiness of love.

Significant damage caused by Childhood Emotional Deprivation

Ways in which emotional deprivation manifests itself in intimate relationships

Childhood emotional deprivation: long-term emotional fallout

Developmental Tasks for Survivors who went through neglect and emotional deprivation.

The Journey of Recovery

How to heal from childhood emotional deprivation

In conclusion

INTRODUCTION

Childhood should be a time of joy, love, and safety, where children are provided with the support and nurturing they need to develop into healthy and happy adults. Unfortunately, for many individuals, their childhood was marked by emotional neglect and rejection from unavailable parents, which can leave deep scars that can last a lifetime. Emotional neglect, a form of domestic abuse, can be hard to identify, and its effects can be difficult to overcome.

If you've experienced emotional neglect and rejection from your parents, it's important to know that you're not alone. Many others have faced similar challenges and have found ways to heal and move forward. This book is designed to provide you with practical guidance and tools to help you overcome emotional neglect and rejection from unavailable parents and find self-discovery.

Through the pages of this book, you'll learn about the signs of emotional neglect, how it can impact your life, and the steps you can take to heal from it. You'll also discover practical strategies to help you build stronger and healthier relationships with your loved ones, and learn how to overcome any negative patterns that may be holding you back.

With the help of this book, you'll be able to start your journey towards healing and self-discovery. So, if you're ready to take the first step towards a brighter and happier future, let's begin.

Childhood Emotional Deprivation

Childhood Emotional Deprivation is a term used to describe the lack of emotional support, nurturing, and care that a child experiences during their formative years. Emotional support is crucial for a child's healthy development, and a lack of it can lead to long-lasting consequences on their mental and emotional well-being.

Children who grow up in an environment devoid of emotional support may experience a sense of emotional neglect, which can be damaging to their sense of self-worth and confidence. They may feel unloved, unwanted, and unsupported by their caregivers, leading to feelings of abandonment and isolation. These negative emotions may persist into adulthood, and the child may struggle with developing healthy relationships due to their lack of trust in others.

Emotional deprivation during childhood can have significant implications for an individual's mental health. Studies have shown that children who experience emotional neglect are more likely to develop depression, anxiety, and other mental health disorders later in life. This may be due to the fact that children who are emotionally deprived are more likely to struggle with emotional regulation, self-esteem, and coping mechanisms.

Furthermore, emotional deprivation can also affect a child's brain development. The emotional center of the brain, the amygdala, is responsible for processing emotions and reacting to stress. Children who experience emotional neglect may have an overactive amygdala, leading to an increased response to stress and difficulty managing emotions. This may contribute to the development of mental health disorders, as well as difficulty in social situations.

It is important to note that emotional deprivation can occur in many forms. It may involve a lack of affection, attention, or validation from caregivers, as well as exposure to traumatic events that are not properly addressed. Emotional deprivation may also occur as a result of a parent's mental health issues, substance abuse, or other factors that prevent them from providing emotional support to their child.

In conclusion, Childhood Emotional Deprivation is a serious issue that can have significant consequences on an individual's mental and emotional well-being. It is essential that caregivers provide emotional support and nurturing to their children during their formative years to promote healthy development and prevent the long-lasting effects of emotional neglect.

Neglected children internalize a central message that conveys their insignificance and unworthiness of love. Childhood Emotional Deprivation occurs when parents fail to provide the necessary emotional support for their children. This can be due to a variety of reasons, such as being preoccupied with their own issues, frustrations, or entitlements. Neglectful parenting can also take on more active forms, such as assigning parental responsibilities to the child or suffocating them, which reflects control issues and dependency. Additionally, certain parents may breach boundaries in front of their children by engaging in inappropriate behavior such as substance abuse or illegal conduct, which shows self-absorption and disregard for their children's needs.

Regardless of the form it takes, the common factor in emotionally deprived children is that they are marginalized in their parents' lives. Their basic needs for care, guidance, and protection are often seen as excessive, troublesome, or ungrateful by their parents, who may feel resentful towards them. Negligent parents are often individuals who were themselves neglected as children and did not develop optimally due to their own emotional needs not being met. However, they may not recognize the problem they are transmitting to their own children due to their lack of insight and perspective.

The absence of healthy attention and care causes children to experience fear, lack confidence, feel emotionally insecure, and unloved. Ultimately, emotionally deprived children may develop a sense of worthlessness due to feelings of abandonment. Neglected children may feel like they must serve their parents in a futile effort to gain what emotionally available parents naturally provide: active love and nurture of their offspring.

Significant damage caused by Childhood Emotional Deprivation

Emotional neglect during childhood can lead to long-lasting effects on an individual's emotional well-being. The lack of a stable and secure attachment with parents can result in feelings of worthlessness and chronic fear, which can trigger depression and anxiety related to abandonment. These insecurities can lead to extreme behavior in relationships, such as hyper-independence or clinginess. Individuals with insecure attachment may develop a Dependent or Avoidant attachment adaptation, both of which are rooted in fear. In some cases, individuals may switch between extremes of hyper-independence and anxious clinging, which is referred to as Disorganized attachment or Fearful Avoidant attachment.

Parents who fail to provide emotional support to their children are unable to guide and support them through normal developmental stages. Children require age-appropriate support and encouragement for growth, including appropriate boundaries, structure, and independence. Without these developmental necessities, children may struggle with self-direction and motivation, which can result in difficulties establishing self-sufficient lives as young adults. This phenomenon is commonly referred to as "failure to launch," where individuals remain dependent on their parents or others for an extended period of time.

When children experience emotional neglect, they frequently do not receive the necessary direction and training to care for their physical, mental, and social well-being. This may result in unfavorable consequences as they may have to depend on trial and error or model their actions after unsatisfactory role models.

Insufficient emotional nurturing during childhood can have detrimental effects on an individual's self-worth, motivation, and ability to regulate emotions. The absence of appropriate care can lead to difficulty in managing and expressing emotions, resulting in alternating periods of numbness and overwhelm. The emotional neglect can also create a sense of persistent isolation and abandonment, which may become deeply ingrained and resistant to change. Caregivers who fail to provide proper emotional support may cause individuals to misunderstand and misinterpret emotions, leading to confusion and triggering of emotional reactions. This can result in chronic self-doubt and low self-esteem.

Children who grow up with emotional neglect may develop a tendency to seek out relationships with individuals who are emotionally unavailable or abusive, continuing into adulthood and affecting their choice of partners. This behavior may be due to their upbringing, as they may have internalized a belief that they are not deserving of love and care. Individuals who have experienced emotional neglect may also be prone to codependent or love-addicted relationships with partners who evoke similar abandonment fears. This pattern is known as trauma bonding, where the emotional brain seeks out familiarity to resolve past emotional wounds. However, this can result in further harm when individuals choose partners who replicate the emotional harm inflicted by their primary caregivers, leading to additional emotional distress.

Ways in which emotional deprivation manifests itself in intimate relationships

Emotional deprivation, stemming from childhood experiences, can manifest itself in a variety of ways within intimate relationships. These ways may vary depending on the individual's personality, upbringing, and the specific nature of their emotional neglect.

At its core, emotional deprivation refers to a lack of emotional responsiveness and support from one's primary caregivers during childhood. When such needs are not met, children may develop negative beliefs about themselves, others, and the world around them. These beliefs can shape their behaviors and attitudes towards their own emotions and the emotions of others, often affecting their capacity to engage in fulfilling and intimate relationships.

One common way emotional deprivation shows up in intimate relationships is through the assumption that one's partner can read their mind. When a person has experienced emotional neglect, they may not have learned how to effectively communicate their emotional needs and desires. This lack of communication can lead to feelings of frustration, resentment, and disappointment when their partner does not meet their emotional needs, even if those needs were not explicitly expressed. This assumption of mind-reading can create unrealistic expectations and set the relationship up for failure.

Another way emotional deprivation may appear in intimate relationships is through a facade of strength or confidence that is not genuine. When a person has grown up in an environment where emotional needs are not met, they may have learned to mask their true feelings as a coping mechanism. This facade can make it difficult for their partner to connect with them emotionally and provide the support they need. It can also make it difficult for the individual to be vulnerable with their partner and open up about their true feelings, which is essential for intimacy.

In some cases, emotional deprivation can result in aggression or passive aggression that hides fear-based hurt. If a person experiences emotional abandonment anxiety, they may react by being either angry and demanding or cold and rejecting towards their partner. This behavior stems from the belief that their partner does not care enough about them, perpetuating the feeling of emotional neglect. If left unchecked, these fears can eventually create a divide between the individual and their partner, making it difficult to maintain a healthy relationship.

Finally, ongoing unfulfilled emotional needs may cause a person to become emotionally detached, distrustful, indifferent, and unapproachable in intimate relationships. The constant anticipation of being let down can perpetuate the issue of emotional neglect and prevent the individual from receiving the emotional support they need from their partner. This detachment can make it difficult to form intimate connections and create a sense of loneliness and isolation, perpetuating the cycle of emotional neglect.

Overall, emotional deprivation can show up in intimate relationships in a variety of ways, impacting a person's ability to connect with their partner on an emotional level. It is important for individuals who have experienced emotional neglect to acknowledge the impact it has on their relationships and seek support to overcome these patterns and develop healthier relationship dynamics.

Childhood emotional deprivation: long-term emotional fallout

Childhood emotional deprivation can have long-lasting emotional fallout that affects individuals well into their adulthood. These effects can be wide-ranging and include:

1. **The internal negative voice, often referred to as the "troll":** This is an internal dialogue that can be negative, critical, and harsh towards oneself. This negative voice can be a result of childhood emotional deprivation, as the individual may have internalized the criticism and negative messages they received from their caregivers. For example, if a child was

constantly told that they were "not good enough," they may internalize this message and have a persistent negative self-talk that can affect their self-esteem and self-worth.

2. **A sense of confusion or disorientation resulting from the invalidation of one's own thoughts and feelings:** Children who are emotionally deprived may not have had their thoughts and feelings validated or acknowledged by their caregivers. As a result, they may struggle to trust their own thoughts and feelings in adulthood, leading to confusion and disorientation. For example, if a child expressed sadness or anger, but was told to "just get over it," they may learn to suppress their emotions and struggle to recognize or express them in adulthood.

3. **Negative and false beliefs about oneself:** Childhood emotional deprivation can lead to negative and false beliefs about oneself. For example, a child who is constantly criticized or neglected may internalize the belief that

they are unworthy or unlovable. These negative beliefs can impact their self-esteem and self-worth in adulthood, leading to a lack of confidence and self-doubt.

4. **The individual in a family who is ostracized or perceived as different from others:** Children who experience emotional deprivation may be perceived as different or the "black sheep" in their family. This can lead to feelings of isolation and exclusion. For example, if a child is constantly criticized or ignored by their parents while their siblings receive praise and attention, they may feel like an outsider in their own family.

5. **A persistent feeling of being alone, often without any clear explanation:** Children who experience emotional deprivation may not receive the emotional support and connection they need from their caregivers. This can lead to a persistent feeling of loneliness in adulthood, even if they have close relationships. For example, a child

who was neglected by their parents may struggle to form close connections with others in adulthood, feeling like they can never truly rely on anyone.

6. **Struggles with maintaining self-control and regulation:** Children who experience emotional deprivation may not have learned how to regulate their emotions in childhood, leading to difficulties with self-control in adulthood. For example, a child who was constantly criticized or punished for expressing emotions may struggle to control their emotions in adulthood, leading to impulsive behavior and outbursts.

7. **Difficulty in achieving personal goals or reaching one's full potential:** Children who experience emotional deprivation may struggle to achieve their full potential in adulthood. This can be due to a lack of motivation, self-doubt, and a belief that they are not worthy of success. For example, a child who was constantly criticized or told

they would never succeed may struggle to pursue their goals in adulthood.

8. **Challenges with setting appropriate boundaries:** Children who experience emotional deprivation may not have learned how to set appropriate boundaries with others. This can lead to difficulties in relationships, as they may struggle to assert their needs and preferences. For example, a child who was constantly criticized or had their boundaries ignored by their parents may struggle to set boundaries in adulthood, leading to unhealthy relationships.

9. **A lack of confidence or self-esteem:** Children who experience emotional deprivation may struggle with confidence and self-esteem in adulthood. This can be due to a lack of validation and support from caregivers. For example, a child who was constantly criticized or neglected may struggle to believe in their abilities and worth as an adult.

10.   A strong dependence on others for emotional support and validation:

Children who experience emotional deprivation may develop a strong dependence on others for emotional support and validation. This can be a result of feeling neglected or invalidated by their primary caregivers, which can lead them to seek out validation and support from others. As a result, they may struggle with setting boundaries in relationships, have difficulty saying "no," and may rely heavily on others to regulate their emotions and make decisions.

For example, an adult who experienced emotional neglect as a child may struggle with feeling confident in their own abilities and decisions. They may constantly seek reassurance and validation from their partner, friends, or family members. This can put a strain on their relationships, as their constant need for validation may become overwhelming or suffocating for others.

Furthermore, this strong dependence on others for emotional support and validation can make it difficult for individuals to form healthy, independent relationships. They may struggle with trusting themselves and others, as well as with establishing a sense of self-worth and identity outside of their relationships. In severe cases, this can lead to a cycle of emotional dependency and codependency, where individuals feel unable to function without the constant approval and validation of others.

Developmental Tasks for Survivors who went through neglect and emotional deprivation.

The journey towards healing from emotional deprivation is multifaceted and demands a consistent and determined effort. It entails establishing constructive patterns in the brain and necessitates letting go of resistance while adjusting to new routines and outlooks.

Maturation Skills: To achieve complete recovery from emotional deprivation, it is crucial to address and fulfill the developmental goals that may have been neglected during childhood. These objectives include significant stages in a person's physical, emotional, intellectual, mental, and spiritual development, from infancy to adulthood. Failing to meet these milestones can impede individuals from reaching their full potential and hinder their ability to lead fulfilling lives, both personally and professionally.

Life Skills: Life skills are essential competencies that enable individuals to effectively cope with the challenges and demands of everyday life while achieving personal goals. These skills encompass a wide range of practical abilities and knowledge that are vital for emotional and mental well-being, particularly for individuals who have experienced emotional deprivation. The ability to manage finances, establish healthy habits, maintain good physical and mental health, and practice personal hygiene are all examples of life skills that can help individuals feel more in control of their lives and reduce feelings of helplessness or inadequacy.

By developing and improving life skills, individuals can increase their self-sufficiency and independence, which can be empowering and contribute to a greater sense of self-worth. For instance, someone who has been emotionally deprived may have a hard time feeling capable of managing their finances or establishing healthy routines. However, by learning and practicing these skills, they can gain a sense of control over their life and become more confident in their ability to manage their affairs. In turn, this can enhance their overall well-being and quality of life.

Relationship Skills: Effective interpersonal skills play a crucial role in the healing process for those who have experienced emotional deprivation. Building and maintaining healthy relationships is a key aspect of emotional and mental well-being. Developing healthy boundaries is essential in forming positive relationships with others. It allows us to protect ourselves from being mistreated or taken advantage of by others.

Empathy is another important relationship skill that allows us to connect with others on a deeper level. It enables us to understand and share the feelings of others, which can lead to stronger, more meaningful relationships. Additionally, reciprocity is vital in establishing healthy relationships. It involves both parties contributing to the relationship and supporting each other's needs.

By incorporating healthy interpersonal boundaries, empathy, and reciprocity into our relationship skills, we can improve our emotional and mental health. Setting boundaries helps us focus on building positive relationships with individuals who care for and respect us. Empathy allows us to understand and support others in our relationships. Finally, reciprocity helps us establish trusting, supportive relationships that contribute to our overall growth and well-being.

Personal Development Skills: Personal development skills refer to the abilities and knowledge that an individual needs to improve their overall well-being and achieve their personal goals. These skills involve understanding oneself, managing emotions effectively, and working towards becoming a better person. Self-awareness, self-understanding, and self-worth are crucial aspects of personal development as they help an individual recognize their strengths and weaknesses and build a positive self-image. Emotional self-management involves being able to regulate one's emotions and respond to challenging situations in a healthy and productive manner.

Individuals who have experienced emotional deprivation or neglect may have internalized negative beliefs about themselves, such as feeling unworthy or inadequate. Overcoming false guilt and shame is also a critical component of personal development. By developing skills to recognize and challenge these negative beliefs, individuals can overcome feelings of guilt and shame that may be hindering their healing and growth.

Incorporating personal development skills can be beneficial in the healing process as they help individuals develop a stronger sense of self and become more resilient in the face of challenges. Improving self-awareness, managing emotions effectively, and overcoming negative beliefs can help individuals build a foundation for a healthier and more fulfilling life. By focusing on personal development, individuals can work towards becoming the best version of themselves and achieving their full potential..

Emotional Recovery Skills: Emotional recovery skills involve a range of abilities and strategies that help individuals to recognize, regulate, and recover from their emotional experiences. One key aspect of these skills is self-assurance, which refers to an individual's confidence in their ability to recognize and understand their own emotions as signals of their personal needs and boundaries. This includes being able to identify when their emotions are becoming overwhelming or indicating a need for self-care or support.

Another important aspect of emotional recovery skills is the ability to regulate emotions effectively. This involves learning how to manage intense emotions in a healthy and productive way, such as through mindfulness techniques, relaxation exercises, or seeking support from others. It also includes developing the skills to express emotions in a constructive way, rather than bottling them up or lashing out in an unhelpful manner.

In addition to these skills, emotional recovery also involves the capacity to bounce back from emotional obstacles and challenges. This means developing resilience in the face of adversity, such as through cultivating a positive mindset, seeking out social support, and practicing self-care. It also means learning from difficult emotional experiences and using them as opportunities for growth and self-improvement.

Overall, emotional recovery skills are a critical component of healing from emotional deprivation or neglect. By developing the ability to recognize, regulate, and recover from emotional experiences, individuals can become more resilient, self-sufficient, and emotionally healthy.

Grieving: Acknowledging and working through the absence of supportive caregivers who were needed but not present during childhood is a crucial aspect of healing from emotional deprivation. This process of grieving involves recognizing the impact of their absence and allowing oneself to feel the emotions that come with it, such as sadness, anger, and disappointment. It may also involve mourning the loss of the nurturing and validation that should have been received, but was not. By acknowledging and processing these feelings of loss, individuals can begin to move towards a healthier emotional state and develop a greater sense of self-awareness and self-compassion. It is important to note that grieving is a complex and ongoing process, and may require the support of a therapist or other mental health professional. However, through this process, individuals can begin to let go of the pain and emotional baggage of the past, and move towards a more fulfilling and satisfying life.

Taking care of the inner child: For individuals who have experienced emotional deprivation or neglect, caring for their inner child can be an essential component of the healing process. This involves learning to quiet the inner critic, which can be a persistent and critical voice that may have developed as a result of past experiences. By learning to recognize and manage this voice, individuals can begin to develop a sense of self-compassion and self-love. Reparenting oneself involves learning to provide oneself with the nurturing and supportive care that may have been lacking during childhood. This includes being patient, kind, and understanding with oneself, as well as setting healthy boundaries and developing self-care routines. By taking care of the inner child, individuals can begin to heal from emotional wounds and develop a stronger sense of self-worth and resilience.

The Journey of Recovery

Growing up in an emotionally neglectful environment can impact individuals in both positive and negative ways. It may enhance empathy, insight, and a sense of justice, but it can also lead to emotional wounds such as low self-esteem and unresolved childhood trauma, which can result in complex PTSD or relationship trauma.

Recovering from childhood neglect and trauma is a long-term process that requires emotional support. It is essential to find appropriate social support, especially for those who have never received it before. However, unlike childhood, where parents play a crucial role in developing positive self-regard through loving actions, no one can heal an emotionally neglected adult. Therefore, reparenting oneself is an important process that involves providing the inner child within the adult with love, validation, acceptance, and compassion that they did not receive during childhood.

Reparenting oneself can be a challenging task because the internalized voice of an invalidating or unsupportive parent, commonly known as the Inner Critic or Troll, often dominates and opposes self-nurturance. The Inner Critic takes root in early childhood and operates unconsciously to undermine the child's sense of self-worth by convincing them that they are defective and unlovable. Neglected children are programmed to believe that they are fundamentally shameful, which allows them to justify their parent's neglectful behavior. Abused children protect themselves from overwhelming abandonment terror by blaming themselves and holding onto the false hope that if only they could "fix" themselves, then their parents would come to love them.

It is critical to highlight the harmful effects of this erroneous belief, as it often remains a persistent issue for adult clients. False toxic shame is typically regarded as true, even by reasonable and compassionate individuals, until they start to examine their upbringing critically and question the internalized critic. Therefore, reparenting oneself and silencing the Inner Critic is essential to healing from childhood neglect and trauma. It requires a lot of patience, compassion, and courage, but it is crucial to take the necessary steps towards recovery and leading a fulfilling life.

How to heal from childhood emotional deprivation

To those who have experienced childhood emotional deprivation, I want to offer you a message of hope and encouragement. It's important to know that you are not alone in your struggles, and healing is possible.

First and foremost, it is crucial to acknowledge that the emotional neglect you experienced was not your fault. Children rely on their caregivers for love, validation, and emotional support. When those needs are not met, it can have a lasting impact on their emotional and psychological wellbeing. You deserved better, and it is not too late to give yourself the love and care you deserve.

Healing from emotional neglect can be a long and challenging journey, but it is possible. The first step is to recognize the impact that your childhood experiences have had on your life. It may be helpful to work with a therapist or counselor who specializes in childhood trauma and neglect. They can help you identify and process the emotions and beliefs that have been holding you back, and provide guidance on developing healthy coping mechanisms and communication skills.

It is also essential to build a support system of people who understand and respect your experiences. This can include friends, family members, or support groups. Connecting with others who have experienced similar situations can be incredibly empowering, as it reminds you that you are not alone in your struggle.

As you begin to heal, it is vital to practice self-compassion and self-care. This can involve setting healthy boundaries, practicing mindfulness, engaging in activities that bring you joy, and taking care of your physical health. Remember that healing is a process, and it is okay to take things one step at a time.

It can be challenging to let go of the negative beliefs and behaviors that have been ingrained in us since childhood. However, with patience and persistence, you can learn to re-parent yourself and provide the love and validation that you were deprived of as a child. This involves developing a compassionate inner voice that encourages you to be kind to yourself and validates your feelings and experiences.

Remember that healing is not a linear process, and setbacks are a normal part of the journey. Be kind to yourself and celebrate your progress, no matter how small. You deserve to live a happy and fulfilling life, and with time and effort, you can overcome the effects of childhood emotional deprivation and create a brighter future for yourself.

In conclusion

Coping with the effects of childhood emotional neglect is a difficult journey, but you are not alone. With the information and guidance provided, you can understand your emotions and take steps towards healing. You have the power within you to overcome your past and live the life you deserve. Remember to seek support from others and embrace your strengths. Keep moving forward, and never forget that every small step towards healing is a step in the right direction.

Printed in Great Britain
by Amazon

43262040R00030